Walk

THE SOUTH HAMS

Brian Carter

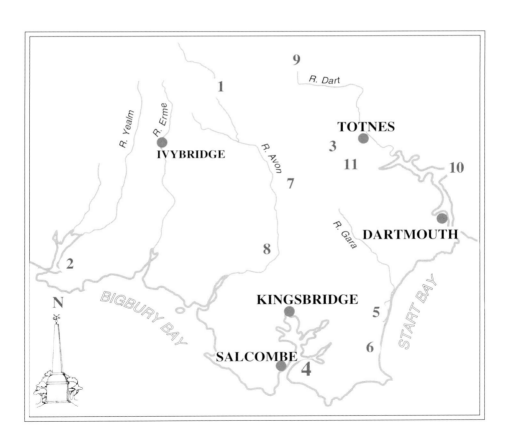

9

R. Dart

1

R. Yealm

R. Erme

TOTNES

3

IVYBRIDGE

R. Avon

11

10

7

R. Gara

DARTMOUTH

8

2

N

BIGBURY BAY

KINGSBRIDGE

5

START BAY

6

SALCOMBE

4

OBELISK PUBLICATIONS

OTHER OBELISK PUBLICATIONS

Places:
(All by Chips Barber)
From The Dart to The Start / Dartmouth and Kingswear
Torquay / Paignton / Brixham
The Great Little Dartmoor Book / The Great Little Exeter Book
The Great Little Totnes Book / The Great Little Plymouth Book
Beautiful Dartmoor / Beautiful Exeter
Torbay in Colour / Plymouth in Colour
Made in Devon (with David FitzGerald)
Burgh Island & Bigbury Bay (with Judy Chard)
Dawlish and Dawlish Warren / The South Hams
Around & About Salcombe / Around & About Seaton and Beer
Around & About Sidmouth / Around & About Teignmouth and Shaldon

Spooky and Mysterious
Tales of the Unexplained in Devon, *Judy Chard*
Haunted Happenings in Devon, *Judy Chard*
Dark and Dastardly Dartmoor, *Sally & Chips Barber*
The Ghosts of Exeter, *Sally & Chips Barber*
The Ghosts of Torbay, *Deryck Seymour*
The Ghosts of Berry Pomeroy Castle, *Deryck Seymour*
The Ghosts of Brixham, *Graham Wyley*
The Ghosts of Totnes, *Bob Mann*
Tales of the Teign, *Chips Barber & Judy Chard*
Weird and Wonderful Dartmoor, *Sally & Chips Barber*
Ghastly and Ghostly Devon, *Sally & Chips Barber*

Dartmoor and Walking
Diary of a Dartmoor Walker / Diary of a Devonshire Walker, *Chips Barber*
Ten Family Walks on Dartmoor/Ten Family Walks in E Devon, *Sally & Chips Barber*
Walks in the Shadow of Dartmoor / Walks in Tamar & Tavy Country, *Denis McCallum*
The Great Walks of Dartmoor / The A to Z of Dartmoor Tors, *Terry Bound*
The Templer Way, *Derek Beavis* / Dartmoor Mountain Bike Guide, *Peter Barnes*
Walking "With a Tired Terrier" in and around Torbay, *Brian Carter*

Acknowledgements
Cover photographs by Chips Barber
Map on title page by Sally Barber
All other sketch maps (not to scale) and drawings by the author

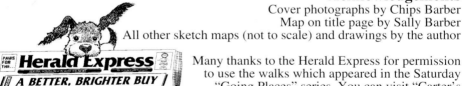

Many thanks to the Herald Express for permission
to use the walks which appeared in the Saturday
"Going Places" series. You can visit "Carter's
Country", Monday to Friday in the Herald Express

First published in 1992, reprinted in 1994 by
Obelisk Publications, 2 Church Hill, Pinhoe, Exeter, Devon
Designed by Chips & Sally Barber
Typeset by Sally Barber
Printed in Great Britain by
Maslands Ltd, Tiverton, Devon

WALKS IN THE SOUTH HAMS

INTRODUCTION — The Lure of the Lanes

I love lane walking and often take off into the South Hams after just a glance at the map. Over the Dart the great plateau is waiting with its river valleys, estuaries, coombes, farms and small communities. And it continues to brew that old red soil magic when cloud shadows glide across the landscape or a village lies beneath the smoke of cottage chimneys.

The seasons touch familiar scenes with beauty from the frost-powdered cabbage leaf, a sea mist snuffing out larksong, to the blackbird singing across the blossom of a cider apple orchard.

Lane walks are the easiest and often the best way of exploring the hidden corners of South Devon, and en route I like to browse around villages, chat to residents, bite into a pie and sample the local cider.

A dose of liberty we took for granted as kids during the school holidays can prove a tonic, and there are plenty of places in the South Hams where you're unlikely to meet other walkers. Purist ramblers who opt for public footpaths, green lanes and moorland ways will probably shudder at the thought of tramping a mile or so beside a busy country road or lingering to enjoy the council house gardens on the edge of a hamlet. But I take whatever a casually planned lane walk gives

me whether it's a glimpse of a fox or a bird of prey or the pasty in the market town delicatessen.

In other words I've become a wayfarer, a pie-and-pint pilgrim, browsing,

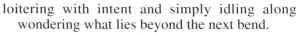

loitering with intent and simply idling along wondering what lies beyond the next bend.

I try to avoid beauty spots while the off-beat attracts me especially if it's off the beaten track. Going alone can be fun but some of my most memorable lane walks have been done with friends. Nothing dampens enthusiasm, however, like the wingeing bloke who moans about everything from his footwear to the weather, has no sense of humour and no genuine appreciation of the joys of lane walking. My companions are fellow rural romantics. They share my love of country pubs which add a warm human dimension to the lane experience. Apart from anything else, my walks are a ceaseless quest for the generous log fire, the perfect bar snack and the sort of cider usually reserved for saints when Peter greets them at the Pearly Gates.

When I began these leaf, mud and birdsong ambles some time ago my evolution as a walker seemed complete or, at least, the wheel had turned full circle. My first real walks as a kid were Sunday afternoon strolls with my parents through the lanes around Torbay. Then I graduated to the coastal paths, the moors, the bigger hills and mountains, preferring solo expeditions to get the maximum out of desolation.

Now, in my mid-fifties, I'm hooked on rediscovering home territory to get a clearer parochial slant on life. Don't get me wrong. I carry little excess weight and haven't lost my appetite for wilderness country. But not so long ago my boyhood love of just ambling off beyond the last houses and allotments was re-kindled. In a sense it was a homecoming.

My walks are more than nature rambles although the song of a blackbird will probably halt me in my tracks for the rest of my life. Hawthorn in blossom is a delight and so is the smell wafting from the chip shop in the country town at dimpsey. I'm hooked on the babbling brook and the bubbling barley wine; swallows around church towers and swallows in public bars; miles, stiles and ripe Stilton; lych gates and lunch breaks; Salcombe smokies and Inch's vintage cider; the prehistoric remains on a hilltop and the remains of pickled onions, a bit of Devon Blue and a bread roll on a plate.

The magic begins with the first step in the first lane, but go with kindred spirits or no companions except the signposts. Leave your mind and heart open and the place will do the rest.

1. A Borderland of Beauty — South Brent and Shipley

Total distance: about 5 miles

"Often and often it came back again to mind, the day I passed the horizon ridge...
To a new country..."

I recalled the first lines of Edward Thomas' "Over the Hills" as I scraped the ice off the car windows and prepared to pick up Ron Walter.

I needed a breath of Dartmoor but a different corner to the familiar places I've tramped since childhood, so we drove to the pleasant village of South Brent and parked outside the Village Hall in Station Approach.

Sunlight flooded a morning of blue sky and frost as we set off from the railway bridge beyond the clatter of a train.

Across the narrow country road The Manor stood in the seclusion of its well-groomed acres and the Avon was rushing through the parkland.

Lane walking often provides panoramic views from gaps in the hedges plus the chance to enjoy the minutiae of hedgebank plantlife. This proved especially rewarding soon after we had turned right at Oakhill Cross with frost riming the wayside leaves.

There among the ferns in the bank two dog violets were in bloom. Saturday January 13, and I had found violets before celandines!

I could imagine Dorothy Wordsworth pointing them out to William and brother and sister marching off into the Cumbrian sunlight as if they had discovered a couple of new stars.

The lovely Avon valley to the left was dominated by the granite outcrop of Corringdon Ball which, if you hate dealing in metres as I do, is 1,092 good English feet high.

This wasn't new country but I had been absent from it for long enough to develop an appetite for that stretch of Dartmoor borderland.

Ron and I came up past ranks of stunted holly trees to Higher Lutton and a crowing cock. Another distinctive rock mass crowned the thousand foot Brent Hill and we were crunching a little cat ice where mud and puddles had frozen, while the lane crept skywards with those gateway cameos of coombes and hillsides to liberate the spirit.

On the horizon wilderness graced the edge of typical hill grazing but across the coombe to the left were small pastures full of sheep, hens and cattle. The sunlight, the cries of birds, the farm animals and the nearby heights of the open moor created the sort of rural idyll that would have brought a smile to Edward Thomas' face.

Ron and I bore left at the cross following the sign marked Shipley Bridge and Didworthy.

Now it was downhill by a modern dwelling tucked away behind high gates with a pair of Doberman Pincers to discourage unwelcome visitors. Presently, though, there was a superb view down a coombe towards the South Hams and a landscape holding the sort of winter sunshine that warms the heart. To the left was Overbrent and a pasture crowded with lambs. Almost opposite Overbrent were Lower Downstow stables and we were striding on beneath an old beech tree fit for angels to roost in. Gorse was blooming and the new-born lambs over the gate wore little transparent plastic macs.

The next uphill stretch brought us beyond Yalland Cross into a vision of fields which had taken on a definite moorland character. The hedgerow banks of earth had given way to stone walls crowned with soil and holly scrub. Redwings settled among the dark leaves and over the coombe neat rectangles of drystone walls advertised the meeting of in-country and bracken moor.

Shipley Tor was the outcrop on the right but before long we were marching down a lane beneath adult oaks and a vaulting of branches and twigs patched with blue. On the other side of the cattle grid we were greeted by the Avon roaring under Shipley Bridge.

Avon comes from the Celtic Afon and means river. I prefer the more ancient name of Aune but the quaint River River probably occurred when the Saxon invader pointed at the river and asked the native Briton for its name.

The baffled aboriginal would have shrugged and said: "Avon - you bliddy girt vool," and so Herr Thick got his River Avon which must have had the locals falling about every time their conquerors said it.

Half a dozen cars were in Shipley Bridge car park with their occupants no doubt treading the well-used trail to the Avon Dam but our way was signposted Didworthy and Aish. Again while Ron and I negotiated the next cattle grid to come on past Zeal and cross the bridge over the Bala Brook, I contemplated the joys of lane walking.

The odd car wasn't a nuisance and we met very few people on foot. Wildlife was constantly making an appearance and the quietude was a nerve tonic.

Walking into the sun we paused to release a sheep that had got stuck in a wire fence before striding on past delightful Zeal Cottage which also had a large dog in its grounds.

Leaving Little Zeal behind we heard the low banjoing of chickens in the nearby paddock and the skirling of the buzzard circling the trees of Didworthy Bottom. Then there was another image straight out of Edward Thomas' verse — three white doves sunning themselves on a slate roof.

After Bridge House, Didworthy Turn Cross convinced us we were on the road to South Brent and even if we had taken the right hand fork to Badworthy and Merrifield we would have eventually returned to our route.

Being fond of South Devon's rivers it was fun to walk above the Avon with the catkins on the hazel twigs dangling perfectly still in the windless air and the river noisy among its boulders.

Passing some frost-starched lawns and Avon Cottage we were rewarded with the spectacle of Brent Hill and the homesteads of Higher Lutton across the valley. A tractor chugged by and there beneath the sunhaze gleamed the rooftops of

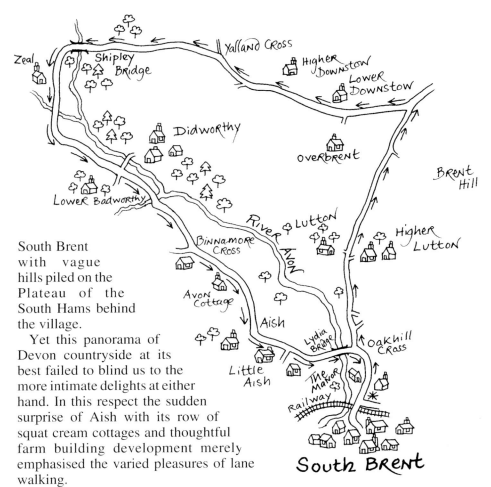

South Brent with vague hills piled on the Plateau of the South Hams behind the village.

Yet this panorama of Devon countryside at its best failed to blind us to the more intimate delights at either hand. In this respect the sudden surprise of Aish with its row of squat cream cottages and thoughtful farm building development merely emphasised the varied pleasures of lane walking.

Oddly enough dogs were barking in Treeby Cattery and the drive leading to the handsome dwelling of Somerswood had me thinking of an Arthurian England which owned more to the Pre-Raphaelites than history

We found the Avon again at Lydia Bridge and could sit on the parapet to watch the water boiling white over two cascades. Then there was the mysterious house called The Rock on the Aune to the left and the walled garden and lawns of The Manor facing it.

Moments later we were back at Oakhill Cross. Another train was speeding past South Brent ruffling the rural calm but only for a moment. The shadows were shortening in the fields and I felt happy as we prepared to go in search of a couple of hot pasties.

2. A Civilised Safari in Newton Ferrers and Noss Mayo

Total distance: about one mile

The South Hams is full of surprises like the two small communities which face each other across the creek on the River Yealm near its estuary.

Ever since I began walking the countryside west of the Dart five decades ago Noss Mayo has fascinated me. Just the name itself is intriguing with its Celtic-Nordic ring. Noss comes from Ness, meaning promontory and is derived from the Old English Naes (headland), Old Norse, Nos, and the Old English word for Nose, Nasu. But why Mayo? Is there any connection with County Mayo in Ireland?

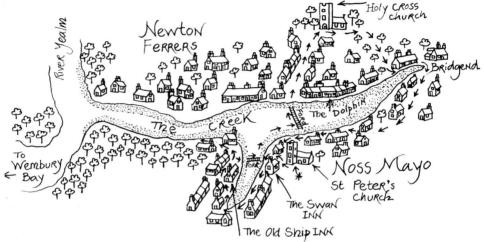

Chris, Ron and I pondered on the mystery as we came down the granite steps into the churchyard of St. Peter Revelstoke at Noss Mayo with the February rain dying around us. On the hill over the creek another church tower beckoned from the trees and between the two towers the tidal mud gleamed grey.

St. Peter's had scaffolding round its steeple and rooks in the Scots pines next to it. One of the deciduous trees brought down by the recent storms had struck the lych gate, buckling the wrought ironwork.

But there was nothing wrong with the granite porch and its lovely vaulting which had a pre-Raphaelite quality. The church may look old but it was only consecrated in 1882 and work was finally finished six years later.

Inside we found a gentle dusk and the eye was drawn to the glow of the stained glass windows. Fortunately there was sufficient light for us to admire the fine woodwork carved by Harry Hams and His Merry Men when the building was new.

After contributing to the Roof Fund Appeal we found a drizzly gloom waiting outside and came under the wonky lych gate down the path and steps on the right to Pillory Hill. Then there was a descent into the woodsmoke billowing off a narrow arm of the creek before we passed Noss Mayo Post Office Stores. Next door stood The Swan Inn and a little further on was a handsome stone house and rows of cottages with a nautical flavour. Small gardens fronted small dwellings.

"There's another pub," Ron said nodding at The Old Ship Inn which graced the waterside over the mud.

Beyond Noss Mayo Methodist Church was a cottage and a jumble of little dwellings, some with half doors, others with the milk still on the doorstep.

Down in the dip at the end of the inlet was the very Victorian-looking Village Hall and on the rise above it Honeysuckle Cottage and a row of white companions stood behind daffodils which bowed in the wind as if it were St. David's Day.

The Parish noticeboard was on our left as we walked up Passage Road by The Tilley Institute to enjoy an amazing parade of cottages. Little porches were reached by flights of steps and some of the windows were shuttered. It would be difficult to conceive anything more Cornish this side of the Tamar. Among them were the irresistible Blue Shutters, Pink Cottage with a dog in residence, and Mariners Cottage. On the shore, The Old Ship Inn was waiting perhaps for the ghost of Long John Silver to come bellowing for his rum. It was a pub no traveller of imagination could divorce from smuggling or a good Stevenson yarn.

Then we reached the wooded section of the Noss and turned back at a little house called The Point. A faint luminosity had crept into the gloom. The tide was out and the mud had a sheen and a nice healthy outdoor stink. By the time we descended the steps onto the beach I was in love with the place.

We crossed the inlet on a causeway of greasy grey stones and waiting on the opposite beach was the roaring wood fire we had smelt on our arrival. In a net loft close by some teenagers were revving up an incredibly noisy motorbike. The snarl dumped me back in the 1990s which, despite cracks in the fabric, could still offer a lot of romance.

Beyond the bonfire was a little jetty called Pope's Quay and steps which led to The Swan Inn.

"Fancy a coffee, dad?" Chris said, but Ron bought them after Chris spilt his loose change all over the bar floor.

"Anything to avoid buying a round," I observed.

If we had wanted ale there was John Smiths on draught which went nicely with the open fire, the snug restaurant and the darts board. But coffee suited the occasion and warmed us for the return to the creek and a short stroll along the shore to another causeway which brought us to Newton Ferrers.

More steps deposited us in Riverside Road West and the beginning of the climb towards the church tower we had seen from Noss Mayo. Near the granite cross a group of residents were discussing the weather and the delightful blue and white Dolphin Inn stood eavesdropping with the cottages in Riverside Road East.

Back on the hill we waved to the friendly looking dog that sat in the window of the house called The Buttery. Then we were among a handful of shops and bungalows ambling on to Newton Ferrers primary school where parents and children were gathering for same sort of occasion.

Bearing right after the school we came past the Court House Hotel to Holy Cross Church and the War Memorial just inside the gate. Inscribed on the granite were the usual sad crop of names but the daffodils and primroses in the churchyard grass were beaded with raindrops and buds were opening on the trees. One gravestone in particular caught our attention, registering like the précis of a family tragedy. James Staddon died Oct 14th 1857, aged 29 years. Susanna Staddon, died Dec 7th 1857 aged 2 years 4 months, and her mother Susanna, the wife of James, died March 31st 1911 aged 80.

The porch invited us into a church full of light and it was pleasant to find parishioners moving around doing small tasks.

Back in the graveyard, with that view to the other tower and the birds singing, I found enough inspiration to feed my animistic perception of God.

Then it was up the road past the geese in the orchard, right at the road island spinney and down the hill signposted Bridgend, Noss Mayo and Stoke Beach. Leaving Barnicott's thatch behind us we came beneath a touch of blackthorn blossom to a ladder set mysteriously against a telegraph pole. Maybe Jacob had climbed up into the sky for a rendezvous with his Maker.

At the creekside the dwellings had evocative names: Wiggle Cottage, Island House and Tides Reach. Before swinging right at Bridgend Cross we nipped over the road for a look at the fine Victorian architecture of Post Office Farm with its multitude of corners and superb porch. Here for the first time since we set foot in the neighbourhood we heard our own accent—Devon wrapped around a suspicious enquiry into why we wanted to know the name of the house.

Returning to Stoke Road we walked back towards St. Peter's Church and passed some old cottages which squatted at the wayside under wooden shingle roofs. A little beyond Smithy Cottage we took the right hand fork for another view of the creek with the tide coming in and the causeway vanishing.

The houses above their steep gardens to the left looked down on this daily coming and going of water and the calls of seabirds and the singing rattle of metal stays against the metal masts of the yachts added to the spectacle.

Gazing over the rooftops to the tower of Holy Cross Church you would have to be a very dull soul not to recognise the magic brewed by the creek. Maybe the rising tide was a metaphor for the living world which continually spilled into the lives of the people of Noss Mayo and Newton Ferrers.

10

3. Mud, Larksong and Cottages — Harberton

Total distance: 2 gentle miles

A patch of blue showed among low clouds as I left the square at Harberton and walked up the narrow road between the Church House Inn and the ancient church of St Andrews. The village is an inviting collection of houses assembled over the years on a hillside surrounded by coombes, hills and copses.

Setting off for Copperthorn Cross I lamented the loss of so many familiar trees in the storms which swept us into the new decade, but that name, Copperthorn, had a lovely ring to it.

Presently I was sauntering past Vine House and a row of stone houses facing the equally handsome Virginia Cottage. At the top of the village in Tristford Road the magnificent old Conservative Club possessed a balcony, a mossy roof and lots of sparrows who were kicking up slightly less din than a House of Commons debate.

More cottages, bearing names like Pump and Woodland saw me up the lane beyond Fairlea to be greeted by the cawing of rooks. The six council houses of Pendarves were a most pleasant surprise for the importance of rented accommodation to village life cannot be over-stated. We need as many repositories for the Devon accent as possible.

The hill climbed between hedgerow banks of primroses and snowdrops and the wind chimes hanging on the front door of the Vicarage rang descant to the cawing of the rooks in the giant conifers at Gills Cross. One of the storm victims was leaning against a sturdier companion but the rooks had not abandoned its top branches.

Then there was a larch plantation on the right and open fields to the left, the greenness broken by farmsteads. West Lodge stood at the gateway of the drive leading to Tristford House and I had a peep at Tristford's strange tower before returning to the lane and the ascent.

It was a real Devon hill rising to 530 feet at Copperthorn Cross and it carried me into larksong. Stopping on the brow to rejoice in the remarkable panorama of farmland sweeping vague to Dartmoor, I also tried unsuccessfully to find the cross. But the cart track was under the brow of the hill to the left as I came down, and the sight of Belsford in the coombe reassured me. Then I found myself treading the Primrose Trail, the hedgerows at either hand thick with the little yellow flowers that brighten Westcountry winters.

In the neighbouring field a harrow rattled over the plough but the countryside was too wet to yield dust and here and there the track itself was boggy and flooded. This definitely wasn't a place for those who sport Hush Puppies or dislike a bit of dirt.

A very muddy stretch found me paddling ankle deep in trainers which are so disreputable my Jack Russell attacks them when I leave them lying around. But it was good to walk between fields with birds busking in the wayside trees.

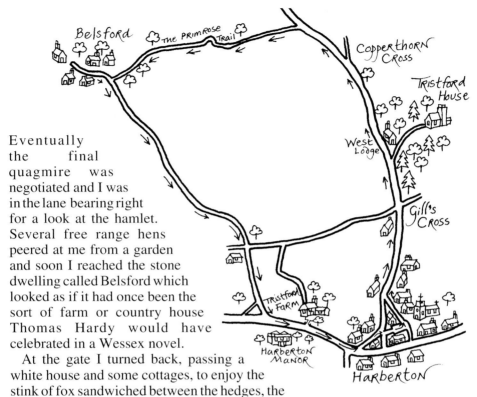

Eventually the final quagmire was negotiated and I was in the lane bearing right for a look at the hamlet. Several free range hens peered at me from a garden and soon I reached the stone dwelling called Belsford which looked as if it had once been the sort of farm or country house Thomas Hardy would have celebrated in a Wessex novel.

At the gate I turned back, passing a white house and some cottages, to enjoy the stink of fox sandwiched between the hedges, the clamour of domestic geese and the clappercawing of the rooks, which seem to be present in large numbers between the Harbourne and the Dart.

Beyond a small linhay, which was the sort of residence a pair of barn owls would consider desirable, another steep hill made me earn my next classic landscape view. I stood on the top by some stables, sharing the vision with a couple of chestnut horses and the larks.

Then I came down, with Harberton visible once more, to Triangle Cross and the left hand fork onto the road which returned me to the village. Harberton Manor, with its classical lines and impressive portico, stood on the right in leafy seclusion. Over the road was the homelier architecture of Tristform Farm and spring flowers massed in the margins of its lawn.

Presently the wayside banks of daffodils opened onto the little cottages of Wesley Place and there was a nice old dog meditating on the road where I turned left opposite Preston Farm.

Facing them, St. Andrews Cottages were also statements of an architectural style that is as South Hams as the landscape itself.

The church clock struck eleven and presently I was back at the Square and the pub with a gentle two mile saunter under my belt.

4. Above and Beside the Salcombe Estuary

Total distance: 3 miles

I left the car on the hill near the hairpin bend at East Portlemouth, high above Salcombe Harbour and the numerous creeks and inlets which make this such a fascinating place.

Salcombe was a short ferry trip away over the water and the houses covering the hillside represented the South Hams at its most picturesque.

But I wasn't looking for picture postcard views as I climbed the hill past the stores and Village Farm to Portlemouth Methodist Church and the Anglican church of St Winwalloe.

To have forsaken the sun and breeze on such an April morning would have been sacrilege so I put the churches, the nursery garden and the squat functional village hall behind me and let the countryside present its surprises.

Opposite the sort of corrugated barn that no landscape deserves, an alarmed cock pheasant scampered through a gate into a field. Meanwhile, the wind in the telephone wires was producing the music of remote countryside.

At Holset Cross I walked left and rescued a caterpillar from the surface of the lane. Then my route had that "up in the sky" feel about it. Animals were grazing the pastures and the occasional gleam of rooftops reminded me of how man had shaped this landscape and was continuing to do so.

This was turning out to be a walk of grand views but the breeze was chill and despite the sun I didn't want to linger even when the lane dropped to bring me into Holset. The hamlet was a scattering of cottages centred on the all too familiar barn conversion of Holset Court.

With its breeding habitat vanishing throughout England, will the 1990s prove to be the twilight of the barn owl?

It was something to brood about as I took the bend and paced on above the ponds of what looked like a fish farm. The downhill stretch carried me into the wind chill again but on the left was the consolation of scrub woodland. The hillside was bright with blackthorn blossom and flowering gorse and a narrow stream ran alongside the lane.

When I'm lane walking I rarely ignore the plant life in the hedgerows and the banks at either hand were a floral delight. Among the bluebells, violets and primroses was a solitary purple orchid. Pausing to admire it I enjoyed a chirping conversation with a willow warbler that couldn't work me out. Maybe he was ready to quit his territory with warblers my size muscling in!

A little later I had a similar whistle-and-chirp chat with a chiff-chaff and could hear St Francis chuckling.

The lane was a gentle nature trail beside a coombe which had been smuggled out of my childhood. Below the high steep banks of gorse and thorn were boggy hollows, thickets of willow and goat sallow and stretches of flags and reeds. Had it been close to Torbay some busybody would have labelled it untidy and demanded it be put to good use.

But these corners of apparent neglect are of vital importance to wild plants and creatures. Argue against species selfishness and your opponents insist you're unrealistic, but species selfishness could cost us everything — and bring the rest of creation to its knees.

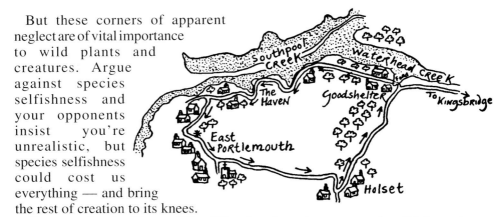

The attractive dwellings of West Waterhead caught my eye and so did the notice on the gate: Slow! Blind dog. Of course I had to crouch and make a fuss of an old rough-haired mongrel who was as gentle as my granddaughter.

On ran the lane and I passed the boat builders before turning left at Goodshelter Cross along the road signposted East Portlemouth. In a dip the way looped around the old ford beside Waterhead Creek and saw me into the hamlet of Goodshelter. Then it was uphill once more to exchange greetings with two friendly children on two friendly ponies. The creek was visible through a screen of hedgerow trees.

A long descent deposited me at the heel of another small inlet called The Haven where some thatched cottages were breathing the foreshore mud. At the wayside further on was a little unattended stall loaded with fresh farm produce. A sign read: Please put money in box.

More thatch waited beyond The Rectory and there was a rookery in the trees on the bend as I came uphill towards my starting point past bungalows displaying nautical names. The sun shone, the wind blew and down below the blue creeks lay between hills which were showing the bloom of spring.

5. The Bay, Leys and Country Ways — Torcross and Slapton

Total distance: just over 6 miles

We set off from the Sherman tank which is a memorial to the American servicemen who died in practice assault landings on Slapton Sands in 1944.

The Lower Ley, part of a long lagoon of freshwater running parallel to the beach, is a bird watcher's paradise and the twitchers were already out in force; but Ron and I were there for everything the morning could offer from gulls to guest houses, cats, cows and cottages, hawks, hamlets and hawthorn and a pleasant stroll through the lanes and back along the edge of Start Bay.

The village of Torcross was a little jumble of guest houses, cafes, hotels and private residences as close to the sea as a community can get. On the corner a lot of ducks had gathered, lisping professionally for handouts. Passing Mr. Hannaford's butcher's shop we watched the pochard diving out on the ley. A screen of reeds and flowering scrub willow stood between us and the calm waters. Echoing that peacefulness were Florence Cottages, built over a hundred years ago in warm stone with porches that were exactly right.

Torcross Chapel and three good looking houses brought us to Leacliff Cottages, also built in 1880 by stone masons who obviously knew their craft. Meanwhile, on the other side of the road, beyond the reeds, a raft of pochard and tufted duck provided a gentle cabaret for passing motorists.

Leaving the ley we walked past Stokeley Barton, Stokeley and Turnpike Cottage to bear right into Kiln Lane and the countryside. It was good to turn our backs on the swish of traffic and enter the sort of hush that the soul needs every so often. Sadly the storms had dropped a giant conifer in the field on the left; but the copse to the right appeared to have escaped lightly and the discovery of that delicate little white flower, stitchwort, in the hedge bank registered as a real triumph.

Then we were among Stokenham's bungalows and their lawns and bird tables, and on the bank on the corner were several shiners — large slabs of slate, quarried locally, and set upright, edge-to-edge, to separate fields. Once a feature of this part of the South Hams, they are now uncommon.

Swinging up the hill we could look back over the rooftops to the church before passing the lane leading to Old Quarry Farm saluted by the bleating of lambs and stereophonic larksong. The sight of an old building, which was an animal house, spiced the characteristic hilltop view and we came by the entrance to the drive of France Farm and down towards a huddle of buildings in a coombe.

The cirl bunting in the wayside tree was friendlier than the workdogs which barked at us outside some attractive byres.

Presently Frittiscombe Lodge, Barn Court and Frittiscombe Farm were behind us and, turning right at the road, we could look over the hedge to Start Bay and the Mew Stone. Slapton village and Slapton Ley were also visible across sheep-dotted pastures; and coming downhill it was apparent that the South Hams was a plateau intersected by long deep coombes.

Stopping at the entrance to Darnacombe Farm we admired the houses and gardens in the coombe below. Moments later Mr. Gilbert Palmer, who has farmed Darnacombe for 30 odd years, drove up on his tractor with his six year old collie cross, Scamp.

It would be hard to conjure up a finer example of the red soil Devonian, a man who has spent a lifetime in agriculture. He spoke of the old days in the old accent and while he talked his fingers idled over his dog's head and ears, and she gazed up at him from a mixture of loyalty and affection.

Mr. Palmer recalled the evacuation of this part of the South Hams at the end of 1943 when the land become The Assault Area where American servicemen practised warfare using live ammunition.

Wishing him well we wandered down to Deer Bridge and a stream cutting through wetlands choked with reeds, scrub willow and alder. It was good snipe country but up the hill at Townsend Cross, Slapton village was waiting and we walked left past a row of cottages and down to another left hand turning. Farm buildings and conversions shared this corner of Slapton with up-market residences. Then there was a pink cottage and a thatched cottage sporting a thatched porch. Big gardens provided plenty of green spaces and above the rooftops ahead a rookery supplied the rural finishing touch.

Up a side alley Ron and I found the delightful little black and white Tower Inn and its courtyard beneath the ruined chantry tower of the old monastery. The inn offers a range of eight real ales and an imaginative menu with Italian food a speciality.

But Sunday morning was a couple of hours off noon and the congregation were enjoying the service in the Church of St James the Great. The steeple pointed at the sky as if the answers to all life's riddles lay in that direction and not through the porch.

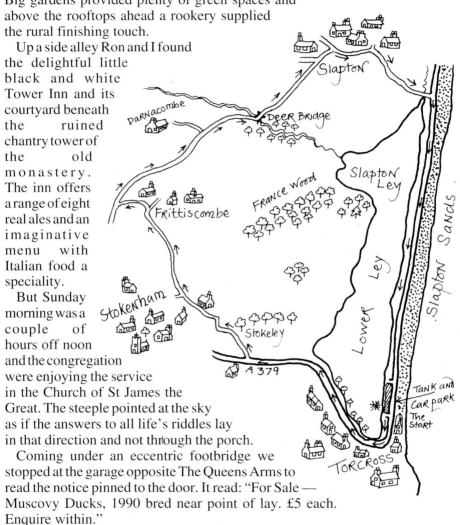

Coming under an eccentric footbridge we stopped at the garage opposite The Queens Arms to read the notice pinned to the door. It read: "For Sale — Muscovy Ducks, 1990 bred near point of lay. £5 each. Enquire within."

A cheerful man grinned through his beard and told me to rush as there were only 90 left!

The Queens Arms looked a friendly pub and one that knew how to cater for the traveller — judging by the variety of Sunday lunches chalked on the blackboard.

We walked down the hill and the right hand bend led us to some more fine stone

16

cottages and houses like Sunny Side. Church Wells was clothed in ivy and the chatter of sparrows, and Rosevine had a blossoming magnolia in its garden. The Willows was cream and green with porches, and the white cottages nearby had blue paintwork while Vale cottages were thatched.

Village architecture always has its surprises and most of the older buildings are a celebration of individual taste and design for living on the human scale.

Turning back we come up past the post office and rookery to Slapton Ley Field Centre and walked out of the village.

It was good to stride towards Start Bay with Start Point jutting into the sea beyond Torcross to the South and the Mew Stone away to the north and the bulk of Froward Point silhouetted behind it.

Slapton Ley was waiting and the birders' cars were lined up in the carpark.

Stopping on the bridge we gazed across the water to the mass of willow catkins, flags and reeds. Presiding over the calm was the song of cettis warblers and the quacking of ducks.

The path to the right ran beside the road and we spent an amusing five minutes spotting the twitchers as tufted duck splashed down and sunlight flashed on binocular lenses. There were birders to the right of us and anglers to the left of us, with cars emerging from the heatdance.

Reed buntings skipped about in the bramble tangles and among the dandelions at our feet were the first sea campions of the year.

All the way back to the tank the rising breeze, the sun and the glitter of the sea and the Ley, and the coming and going of birds lent majesty to the morning.

It was good to be part of it all on the threshold of the Vernal Equinox.

6. The Storm Battered Coast — Start Point and Hallsands

Total distance: about 3 to 4 miles

We left Start Point car park in the teeth of the easterly gale that was flinging waves at the cliffs below. Gulls were airborne, showing off their amazing flight skills, as we walked the coastal path north to Hallsands.

It was a morning of sunhaze and surf thunder, and while Ron lit a cigarette I looked back at Start Point and the lighthouse. The shores of Start Bay are magical at anytime of the year but with spring conjuring up more and more wild flowers and blackthorn still in blossom, the coastline was like a vast theatre about to raise the curtain on an extravaganza that never dates.

The goat-track of a path brought us across the primrose steeps, under the natural arch of a blackthorn and on through a wind-sculpted copse of flowering wild cherry into Hallsands South. The fishermen who once lived in this little shoreline community planted their potatoes in the coombe and cropped the wild cherries from the trees on the hillside.

Bearing right past the holiday apartment we came down to the old village. The danger notices at the wayside were the epilogue of the sad story of the community which built its cottages too close to the sea.

Hallsands South was destroyed in the Great Storms of 1917 but the ruins still hold more than the shadows of how things were. The rollers pounding the shells of former dwellings were like an action replay of the disaster.

The waves continued to rumble in and spindrift was flying as we came back to the holiday apartments and made our way to Hallsands North where a bit of a car park and a 'conservation pond' have replaced the original wetland.

The Hallsands Hotel had lost its roof but still looked sturdy and defiant on the bluff, and I daresay the ale and cider tasted as good as it did on my previous visit.

Above it the sky was littered with jackdaws and surf was creaming over the beach when we turned left at the ley which is choked with osiers and reeds. The lagoon was formed when big seas heaped up the pebbles and shingle on the beach, blocking the stream which flows down the coombe. Unlike Slapton and Widdicombe leys it has half dried out and little water is visible. The reeds provide shelter for migrants like wheaters, sand martins and warblers when they gather here in the autumn. There were more houses and bungalows in Hallsands North than I had imagined when I left the coast. Most of the dwellings were low down the hillside, overlooking the reed beds and scrub willow. It was a delightful place. Walking between banks speckled white with wild garlic flowers we approached the tiny hamlet of Bickerton; and at the bottom of the hill found a notice BEWARE — TOADS CROSSING.

Whenever I come upon evidence like this of people caring for so called "lowly creatures" I feel we've taken a big step on the return to Eden.

It would also be heartwarming to see notices beside the busiest country roads and lanes telling motorists: BEWARE — Low Flying Birds. Throughout the late spring and summer too many fledglings are killed as they flutter between hedges, often on their first flight.

A row of cottages with roofed doors brought us to a beautiful lane above a broad deep coombe. Strolling along, out of the wind, I considered one of the things about South Devon that beguiles me. Born close to Tor Bay at Paignton I am unhappy if I'm away from the sea for very long and in the South Hams the farmland runs to the shore or cliff edge and it is possible to stray from the spectacle of fulmars on the wing into the vision of a buzzard circling a copse.

That combination of earth, sky and water changes throughout the year, and I can't imagine life without it.

At Bickerton Top Cross the wind freshened and hedgerow leaves caught the sun in gleams, juggled it and discarded it, only to catch it again. By now the lane had given way to a road which we tramped in the direction of Start Point, then it was good to stride along the high catwalk, looking across the hills to distances which crumbled and were lost in a mist of sunlight.

By Hollowcombe Head Cross a flock of meadow pipits dashed low over the plough and, beyond the masts of the W.T. Station, Start Farm lay in a goyal.

Moments later we were back at the car, closing the doors against a wind with an icy edge.

7. Of Coombes and Copses — East of Diptford

Total distance: just less than 3 miles

The buzzard laid its cat calls on the windwashed sky but the hawk remained out of sight as Chris and I left Beenleigh Turn Cross. Showers were sweeping in from Dartmoor followed by bursts of sun and a glitter which can make certain landscapes irresistible.

The signpost pointed us towards Beenleigh and the lane was a low-hedged aisle into the sort of South Hams beauty that inspires spiritual well-being.

Less obvious plant life on the hedgebanks was tiny and green — leaves of penny wort, ferns, goosegrass. Photosynthesis produces its poetry year in year out and nature remains indifferent to our response. Certainly it was easier to notice the white and blue bungalow and the free range fowls than the wayside primroses.

Weaned on headlines we have forgotten how to read the small print; but when the firework display is over, the cup final has come to an end, and the Great Storm has blown itself out, the blackbird will sing from the top of your apple tree.

We walked under the power cables by the pylon, listening to the hum of 33,000 volts. Then we were striding past a barn of asbestos sheets and corrugated iron, with a bony Friesian in the yard and Longpark bungalow on the left. Maybe the cows huddled against the hedge in a field of mud had not heard the weather forecast which had put its money on sunny spells and showers, or maybe they had and were investing in bovine instinct.

Water gurgled free alongside the lane and, guarded by a couple of tractors, we found the old byres, barns

To Harberton

Stert Mill

Thorn Farm

Stert Barn

Christonre Cross

The Old Stables

Stert Barton

To Diptford

Blakewell

Beenleigh Farm

Beenleigh Turn Cross

Simpson

To Moreleigh

and stables of Beenleigh Farm. The house itself was cream and blue rural yesterday with a kingfisher blue porch and snowdrops and violets over the way.

"A trailer for the main attraction on general release after the Vernal Equinox?" Chris grinned.

A collection of newer outbuildings sent us to the little stone bridge spanning a stream in the hollow where we bore left in the direction of Harberton. Then it was uphill between steep banks covered in masses of periwinkles. This frail blue flower defies the harshest winter weather but along with the mated songbirds, the hedgehogs which haven't hibernated and the spawning frogs and toads it must have forgotten what a cold snap is.

Beyond the iron ladder standing against the wayside tree were the outbuildings, cattle yards and handsome cream and white house of Thorn Farm.

A shower fell and we came left at the fork to run an eye over the cattle and the sheep with their lambs. Down below, a coombe provided an auditorium for the rooks.

Ambling under a storm-ravaged oak we took a sharp left-hand bend and made the lane descent to Stert Mill which is a private residence of weathered grey stone. The stream was brim full, daffodils nodded and swayed like they eternally do in the Wordsworth poem and there were snowdrops on the banks.

Rain began to fall again but changed its mind and we jogged up the hill to delight in the ivy-clad linhay which registered as perfect barn owl habitat.

A gang of very muddy calves regarded us in silence from their pen in front of the inevitable huge draughty shed which resembled a warehouse. The house called The Old Stables had an unusual section of breeze blocks in its old stone wall but at the back was an attractive walled garden complete with ornamental wrought iron gate.

The farmhouse of Stert Barton was glorious and I passed thinking of the family life it must have fostered, generation after generation, decade after decade.

A nice uphill haul beside a beech hedge brought us eventually to a natural vantage point where it would have been sacrilege not to have paused to admire the view.

If I am forever rejoicing in the South Hams countryside it is because it has the power to draw me into its serenity. Between the fields and copses were solitary farmsteads and small groups of dwellings with everything gentle on the eye.

The long beech hedge led us up into the next shower past the skeleton of barn, a modern house and a converted farm building which I presume is Stert Barn. Finding so many conversions in progress all over South Devon I have to ask if the pursuit of the rural idyll will cost us the barn owl. Wouldn't it be wiser to search for a vacant property in the country than gobble up bits of farm at the expense of this beautiful creature? Perhaps the environmentally conscious South Hams will make a positive stand on the issue, unhindered by central government.

Where the hedge ended the countryside rolled and dipped to the far horizon. Across it columns of rain made their stately progress. It was a good ending to the walk.

A few moments later we were at Christone Cross bearing left along the road back to our starting point, glad to have rekindled a little wonder.

8. Loddiswell and the Wooded Avon Valley

Total distance: 9 miles

We put the car in the free car park at Loddiswell and turned left along South Brent Road past The Loddiswell Inn.

The parish church of St Michael stood behind a cluster of houses, north of the village, and Ron and I came by the London House Stores to Elliott's grocers shop for homemade pasties.

Then New Street brought us past the Congregational Church, with low cost homes being built over the way, and on down the hill.

The April morning held the faint threat of rain. The wind was cool and clouds were massing over the South Hams.

Beyond Great Gate Farm was the lovely Avon Valley, its beauty tarnished by the storm damage to Rake Wood. About 75 per cent of the mature deciduous trees had been brought down and although the spectacle of devastation has become familiar it still saddens me.

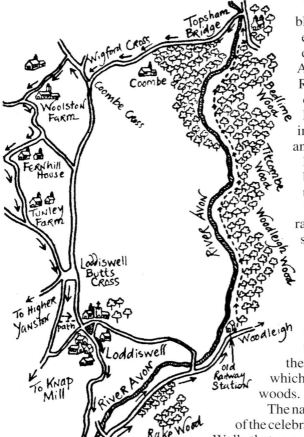

The road was busy, but the bluebell slopes of the wood at either hand made it a pleasant enough descent to the River Avon and New Bridge with Rake Corner Cross waiting on the other side. Bearing left we walked a quieter road in the direction of Woodleigh and Preston, beside the wheat, leaving New Mill Bridge behind us for a close-up of the scarred Rake Wood.

Through the deep coombe ran the Avon and we were suddenly confronted by the little granite gem of Loddiswell railway station. Alas, the line has been long out of use but the public footpath runs beside it and anyone with romance in their soul can only lament the loss of the steam trains which once thundered through the woods.

The narrow path was the beginning of the celebrated Avon Valley Woodland Walk that wound among summer-leafing trees and carpets of bluebells and ramsons (wild garlic). Wherever there was a patch of boggy ground, flowers of marsh marigold were clustered, bright yellow, and the Woodland Trust had laid duck boards. No doubt this is an extremely popular walk and erosion by human feet could be a problem. The wood anemones and masses of white ramsons were a delight matched by the bird song, the sound of the river and the railway bridge with its superb brickwork.

Presently we were walking the banks of the Avon, our nostrils full of the stink of wild garlic.

The river glided by over rock-littered shallows and beyond a stone stile in a stone wall another railway bridge displayed brick slew arches.

The next stile saw us briefly onto the track which once carried the rails. Below the bridge we swung right beside a meadow with the wayside willow full of long-tailed tits and coal tits.

At the "Private" notice on the tree we made a left-hand return to the Avon, scolded by a pair of goldcrests. Alongside the river was a plantation of eucalyptus "whips." The leathery leaves had an alien feel and I was glad when the path deposited us on a narrow country road to bear left past some small dwellings to Topsham Bridge.

On our journey up the Avon Valley we had come through Woodleigh, Titcombe and Bedlime Woods. Once over the bridge and past the old level crossing and what used to be the crossing keeper's cottage, it was lane walking again, up into the smell of wild garlic.

The climb through the conifers was long but I often wonder why this sort of walking does not appeal to more people. Since boyhood I've found it most rewarding, with private viewings of the seasons at work on farmland which is a great, free safari park crowded with British wildlife.

After Coombe Farm (misspelt Combe on the Ordnance Survey map) we came to Coombe Cross and bore right with the intention of avoiding the main road back to Loddiswell.

Soon the signpost marked Loddiswell Vineyard sent us left beyond Wigford Cross, between high banks and beech trees into rich, rural smells.

But we never reached the vineyard.

Leaving Woolston Farm we swung left down a lovely rough lane, then right by the rough old sign which read "Fern Hill House." It was developing into a walk as convoluted as the Celtic mind, but we had no complaints. Even when we were forced to climb onto the hedge to let a big lorry pass our enthusiasm wasn't diminished.

Ignoring an awful building, we looked down into a coombe which sheltered a pond, a walled garden and splendid Alleron House. It was a corner of England Tom Jones (the eighteenth century English scallywag, not the twentieth century Welsh warbler) would have appreciated.

Tunley Farm had calves, byres, barns, an orchard and a really friendly young work dog which we were rag-roustering when the rain started to fall.

At the next hilltop we bore left at a mysterious notice which simply stated "Lavinia's."

"Lavinia's what?" I asked, but Ron refused to speculate.

Other hedgerow signs pointed at invisible B and B accommodation but at Loddiswell Butts Cross the signpost sent us right then left for Knap Mill and the back way into the village.

Walking the quiet road we found a badger sow lying dead on the verge. I hope she died swiftly when the car hit her. Someone with a heart had laid bluebells on the body and I added a bunch of stitchwort. The light had vanished from her eyes but it would shine from the eyes of every creature born this spring.

A handful of bungalows concealed the footpath on the left that led into Loddiswell through a housing estate. A blackbird was singing from a cottage garden and we were back in the small community on the hill above the Avon.

9. The Columbine Triangle — Rattery and Buckfastleigh

Total distance: 11 miles

Leaving the carpark by Rattery Church we came right into Totnes Road to saunter through the village before taking the first turning left to begin the lane walking.

The morning was grey and cool after a brief soak of rain but the dead mole was blind to all. Ron gathered it from the dust and we gave it a Red Indian burial in a wayside tree. My son, Chris, had grown up with this ritual and nodded his approval.

Goats and chickens shared the pasture behind the screen of hazel and hawthorn which often met the hedge opposite halfway above the lane to form one of those leafy naves which lead into spring.

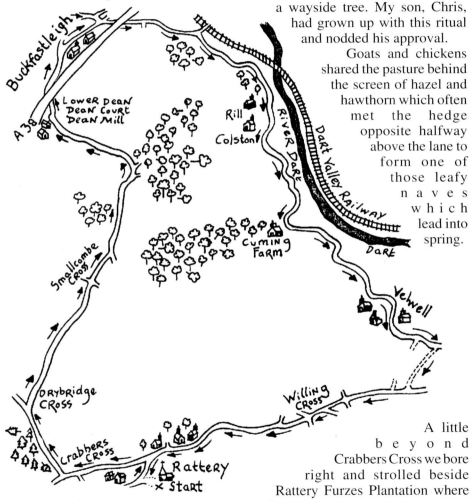

A little beyond Crabbers Cross we bore right and strolled beside Rattery Furzes Plantation where the lane had became a generous country road.

The flowers of May stood in the hedges and there was a lot of blue among the yellows, white and pinks. At Drybridge Cross it was right again by the metal gate into the traffic din rising from the A38. Even the greyness which had crumbled to a mist could not diminish the beauty of the hill country on the left. In fact it accentuated that dimension of mystery which Dartmoor usually reserves for Autumn.

The bungalow called Moorhaze had captured the essence of the occasion in its name but a pair of herons flapping overhead strengthened the magic and then there were the hedgebank columbines, deep violet or pink, the perfect prelude to summer. Near Smallcombe Farm a yellowhammer was singing as we came straight over Smallcombe Cross to bear left at the road which presented us with a marvellous, misty panorama of South Devon hill country.

The wind and the leaf rustle fed that sense of being in nature that is a spiritual tonic and I was pacing through memories when we put Pennywell Farm Centre behind us to stride downhill with the vision of moorland lost in the bottom of the sky calling us on.

The descent carried us towards the roaring A38, past Dean Court bungalow and the orchard beyond Old Buckfastleigh Racecourse to the huge farm outbuildings of the rural complex embracing Lower Dean, Dean Court and Dean Mill. Presently the road ran under the A38 and the thunder of continuous traffic and we bore right on the other side towards Buckfastleigh.

At the George Inn we were scolded by an anxious starling mum who had a nest full of chicks under the eaves. Then some fine little houses led us into the small Dartmoor town where we bought hot pasties at Buckfastleigh Bakery. The Saturday morning bustle was growing when we walked down the street and turned night at the Fruit Basket to come into the Narrows of Elliott Plain.

Over the road, where the houses ended, was Elliot Plain Cross and our route was signposted Beara, Colston, Luscombe and Velwell.

Now Old Totnes Road passed below the A38 through a kind of rustic suburbia before we swung right into Colston Road at the wheelie bins to enjoy lane walking once more.

As the way climbed between nutbushes we could look down on the Dart through the trees to the left. The "River of Oaks" was low. Beyond it was Dart Valley Railway and the A384 — the road most people travel unaware of the quiet places over the Dart.

After Rill Farm there were the water meadows and a sky full of swifts, swallows and house martins, taking insects on the wing. House martins had nested in the eaves of thatched Colston Cottage and cider apple orchards offered the last of their blossom to the bees.

It was turning out to be a beautiful up and down walk with a cock crowing beyond Beara Farm and another steep descent to Cuming Farm before we trudged up a steep hill through the stink of wild garlic.

Passing a neat modern house named Thistlemuir we came under the crackling power cables by the pylon with the round hill of Hood Ball and its trees looking as artificial as a feature in a Boticelli landscape.

More columbines — violet, pink and white — decorated the hedges and we stopped to enjoy them, glad to be there in that corner of Devon.

The way into Lower and Higher Velwell was dusted with hawthorn blossom and the dead badger lying in the field beside the lane had become one with all Nature.

But the lane, like life, ran on until we took a sharp right turn to trudge up a steep cart track of loose rocks and stones beneath mature hedgerow oaks.

A few primroses were tucked away among the grasses and nettles on the banks and the bluebells and campion betrayed the time of year.

At the top of the track we found the narrow road to Rattery and bore right again to walk the base of the rural triangle above the sort of countryside that would inspire a celt to write a love song.

Where our road merged with another three, beech trees stood around a solitary Scots Pine. Then we had reached Willing Cross and the signpost which read: Rattery and South Brent.

Once more the switchback glided over a green landscape under the grey sky and made a final climb before the steeple of Rattery Church came into view and we were back in the village.

10. On the Cider Apple Trail — Stoke Gabriel

Total distance: about 4 to 5 miles

It must be apparent to my regular readers that I am proud of being a Devonian from the south of the county. The native accent is the product of the climate and it has sunlight, clotted cream and a touch of scrumpy in it.

That Saturday morning in late July, when I was dropped off at the car park used by patrons of the Castle pub and the Church House Inn at Stoke Gabriel, I felt deprived of the red soil burr.

There's not a lot of it about in Paignton so trips to villages are necessary to recharge the spiritual batteries.

I intended looking round Stoke Gabriel before tramping the lanes to Higher Yalberton for some of my favourite scrumpy courtesy of the Churchwards. The quest for cider and a good pub like the Church House Inn to round things off lent magic to the walk long before I set off on the Cider Apple Trail.

Leaving Paignton Road I came left down Coombe Shute past Church Orchard and the lovely old Victoria and Albert Inn and on up through the narrows before the road dropped past cottages in pastel shades, with a glimpse of Mill Pool on the right.

At the bottom of Coombe Shute I turned right where the signpost indicates No Through Road and walked Byter Mill Road uphill once more under villas and bungalows. Someone was playing the piano, one of those sonatas which sit sweetly on a summer afternoon.

Gateway visions of the creek offered the spectacle of a mullet shoal whimpling the surface as the fish fed. Despite walking in shorts and trainers I was hot and it was a relief to get into the shade of the wayside trees. The path narrowed to run down to Byter Mill where water was ghosting over the weir, but a green carpet of weed covered the pond.

It was hedge top roses all the way into the sunlight at Old Forge and Port Bridge Cottage. Taking the Waddeton road I swung left only to turn first right into Whitehill Lane at Well Farm.

Now there were orchards in the coombe and the banks were lined with tall hedges.

Lidstone coombe was bonny. The cider apple trees stood each low hills glided up into the

The lane looped down past where I came as a kid for kestrel's stump of a tree behind it by the gate shade of Whitehill Copse. The green luminosity of sunlight Squirrels scuttled off over wood pigeons crooned

The next hilltop of Yalberton Industrial done without and presently I

side of the stream and heat haze.

the disused quarry eggs, left the great nude and tunnelled on into the passage possessed the held in countless leaves. spindly top branches and from the hush.

presented me with a view Estate that I could have was turning right into Long Road and the comforting sight of more orchards at either hand.

Maybe if I incanted the magic names of the cider apples the industrial estate would suddenly blend with the landscape. "Bloody Butcher, Fox's Whelps, Sheep's Nose, Kingston Black, Grenadier, Slack-ma-Girdle."

At the little bridge spanning Cider Brook I checked the water for pollution from the estate but it seemed clear enough although it

was a trickle of its normal self. Lower Yalberton Road was waiting on the left and soon the coombe of orchards was there over the wall.

Thankfully this rural backwater, typical of what South Devon can offer, could not be described as a beauty spot but for those of us who have the blood it is a heart place. Change its character and we are diminished. In any case the spirit can only take so much loss.

Yalberton Industrial Estate is a reality which could be screened with trees. Meanwhile the march of the factories must be halted and the site contained. I know change is inevitable but so is the unhappiness the process can bring to those who feel at one with a countryside.

Keeping a stiff upper lip I marched to the end of the lane and turned sharp left into Yalberton Road.

Some thatched cottages stood on the right and I was approaching the bridge over Cider Brook into Higher Yalberton. Here you can purchase Churchward's and Hunt's farmhouse cider. Both are excellent and both offer a different challenge to the palate, but I am hooked on Mr Churchward's Devon Mix. It is entirely a personal preference and if I am often singing the praises of this smooth scrumpy it is because I find it delightful with a meal or when I'm flopped in the armchair afterwards. Maybe it's because I was weaned on the stuff.

I departed for Stoke Gabriel. The idea was to walk back the way I had come but I cheated and got a lift to the Church House Inn where the Saturday lunch-time trade was hotting up. Lunch at the Church House can set the seal on a good lane walk and the back bar will supply its own red soil cabaret.

Funny how those Devon accents get broader and broader in the summer but thin a bit towards Christmas!

11. Leaf Shadow Lanes in the Harbertonford Countryside

Total distance: just over 3 miles

Beginning at Harbertonford church I crossed the Totnes road, passed The Maltsters Arms and turned left into Old Road at the bridge spanning the Harbourne.

The Hungry Horse Restaurant faced the Post Office Stores and I came between the cottages to Bow Road where the signpost pointed me towards Tuckenhay and Ashprington.

It was a day of soft cloud, sunshine and a breeze strong enough to lift the fallen leaves. Putting Harbertonford Methodist Church behind me, I slowed down to enjoy the fine brick council houses of Marl Park with their gardens and the washing flapping on clothes lines. I'm always a bit suspicious of villages without council houses but Harbertonford's would be a credit to any rural community.

The opposite side of the country road provided a footpath that followed the Harbourne and I could amble along enjoying the sight and sound of sun-dappled water. This is the river that runs through my novel, *The Moon In The Weir*. Its leaf-patterned shallows held the reflections of trees and clouds and I was poignantly reminded of the otters that live on in the book beyond the reach of time.

No. 20 Bow Road had a garden full of splendid blooms which my old dad would have appreciated. It's some years since he died, but I often feel his presence as I walk South Devon or prop up a bar or catch the red soil accent in one of his favourite haunts. Maybe the magic words will conjure him out of a South Hams' dimpsey: "Do'ee want another pint of rough, buyh?"

Soon the road narrowed to a lane with a hard surface and the river for company. Burna is the Old English name for stream and it is good to find it surviving as bourne (the Harbourne).

Friesian cattle were grazing the water meadow beside the river and in the next field there were fowl and geese. The wood on my left was whispering as I approached Crowdy Mill where a notice informed me I could buy free range eggs, homemade jam and, of course, the celebrated flour.

It was an idyllic little place with the water wheel turning and the Harbourne in close attendance near the leat.

The Cider King

Sheep were lunching on the hillside field across the river and the other pastures were being devoured by cattle. Sharing an Autumn noon with grazing animals is good for the soul and the hawthorn tree I found growing at the wayside brought me to a spiritual high. The hawthorn is my favourite tree although I continue to pay lip service to the cider apple!

I passed the nursery wearing the vacant smile of a scarecrow and gazed down into the tree-choked coombe where willow leaves were whitening in the breeze and the river wound on towards Bow Creek and the Dart.

The lane had become a tunnel through autumn but gateways provided views over the Harbourne to foxy banks and treehackled steeps.

The track to the right dived to Beenleigh but I walked on with conifers to the left and a fine old orchard on the opposite side. The next gate presented me with a vision of red plough curving up against trees and the sky. I swung left ignoring the Ashprington-Bow Bridge sign and allowing myself to be directed towards Luscombe and Totnes.

Prowse's Luscombe is a pleasant house incorporating the old farmyard. Further on ravens were aloft above the orchards and I was walking the hill to the grey stone of Middle Luscombe Cottage, a cluster of out-buildings and the pink-washed walls of the dwelling called Skindles.

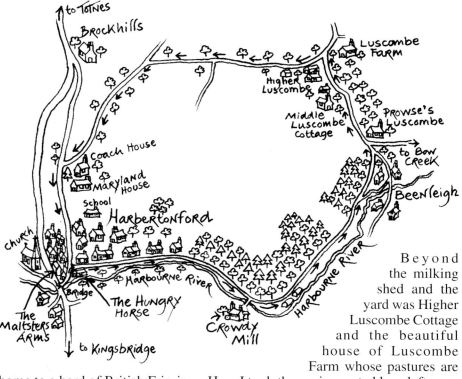

Beyond the milking shed and the yard was Higher Luscombe Cottage and the beautiful house of Luscombe Farm whose pastures are home to a herd of British Friesians. Here I took the unsignposted lane left, up a hill laced with farmyard smells. Presently I had to look back down the coombe of the Harbourne, which must rate as one of the most delightful corners of the South Hams.

I was carrying some of the stiffness, aches and pains of Sunday's soccer but the ascent under tall hedges and ash trees was just what my legs needed.

On the 400 ft summit I changed lanes and bore left to stride into the panorama of hills and coombes which met Dartmoor in the bottom of the sky.

There were enough glimpses of red soil to warm the heart of born and bred

Devonians and I was congratulating myself on re-discovering one of the finest lane walks I've ever taken. The day itself contributed to the experience. Cloud shadows drifted across the countryside, lending it a dreamlike quality. This certainly was Devon at its most glorious, a landscape on the human scale, breathing just enough mystery to make me curious about what lay beyond the horizon.

Another gateway let me look down on the Kingsbridge-Totnes road and Brockhills Farm and the sort of pastoral scene I've celebrated in five of my six novels. Well, the majority of my books have just been excuses to write love letters to ancestral places. Extravagant language? Sure — it has to be to capture the depth of emotion this countryside rouses in me.

Tapestries Coach House was a clean cut white building near the corner where two lanes met and became one to carry me left downhill past Maryland House. A couple of buzzards circled high on the same thermal and suddenly I was looking across the rooftops of Harbertonford. The cries and laughter of children rose from the village school and I paused to chat with a ginger and white cat outside Leigh bungalow.

It was satisfactory to be in one of the older parts of Harbertonford where the tucked-away lanes and drangs led to tiny backwaters. I had an appetite now for some of the things on the menu at The Hungry Horse, maybe the hot cheese and spinach souffle or the baked garlic mussels for starters; but the restaurant opens in the evening so I nipped into the Post Office Stores and got a nice portion of cooked chicken.

I lunched al fresco at the bridge beside the river and washed down the snack with a half of rough at The Maltsters Arms. Classic lane walks should always have a pub at journey's end.

BRIAN CARTER May '91

OTHER TITLES FROM OBELISK PUBLICATIONS

DIARY OF A DARTMOOR WALKER
Chips Barber

Diary of a Dartmoor Walker is a light-hearted book that includes many unusual strolls, rambles, excursions and expeditions in all areas of the Dartmoor National Park. There is the Lich Way, or the way of the dead (and the dying!), the Abbot's Way, the North/South Crossing and even the Tom Cobley Walk. This 'diary' spans the four seasons to capture Dartmoor in a way that no other book has managed so far – and the walks are quite interesting too!

DIARY OF A DEVONSHIRE WALKER
Chips Barber

In this amusing and entertaining book, Chips Barber describes his walks over Dartmoor, the Haldon Hills and along the Devonshire coastline in his own inimitable style. We are confident that anyone who reads *Diary of a Devonshire Walker* will want to get onto the boulder-strewn landscape of the open moors or along the rugged South Devon coastline. This is a walking book with a difference, one that no self respecting lover of the Devon countryside should be without.

BEAUTIFUL DARTMOOR, Chips Barber

Dartmoor is a land often described as England's last great wilderness and there are remote tracts of land where you can wander for miles without seeing another person. In contrast, within its 365 square miles there are popular places where crowds are drawn to savour Dartmoor's unique atmosphere. Chips Barber has compiled over 30 colourful photos to create a lasting souvenir of this magnificent and inspiring landscape.

THE SOUTH HAMS, Chips Barber

The South Hams is one of the loveliest areas in the whole of England. Chips Barber describes a journey around The South Hams which begins at Totnes, then flows down the Dart to Dartmouth. The stunningly beautiful South Hams coastline and the sheltered estuaries which funnel inland are then explored and the villages and towns, all set so superbly into the patchwork quilt of countryside, are all featured. Chips illustrates his book with sketch maps and carefully selected photographs, combined with many fascinating facts and amusing anecdotes.

DARTMOUTH and Kingswear
Chips Barber

Dartmouth may not be very big but most people will know it almost as a household name for it's played a significant part in the history of our nation. This book features some of the more unusual aspects of this South Hams town. Discover the narrowest house in Devon, look for the town's many dragons, hear how it's a lot closer to Aberdeen and the Amazon than you may think, enjoy a few walks and see why it has been described as the prettiest place in the world!

FROM THE DART TO THE START
Chips Barber

This stretch of the South Hams coastline has its own unique past. Apart from the disaster which befell the small village of Hallsands, near Start Point, and the tragedy of the American troops rehearsing for D-Day, there is also much more lesser known history to discover. Read about the last, ill-fated highway robbery ever committed in this country, and the submarine that was all at sea until it was passed by a cyclist! Featuring many more unusual tales from this lovely area, it covers Stoke Fleming, Strete, Slapton, Stokenham, Torcross, Beesands, Hallsands and Start Point, where it finishes!

BURGH ISLAND AND BIGBURY BAY
Chips Barber / Judy Chard

This little book is packed with stories and is the perfect informative souvenir of any visit, however brief. Ghost stories, disasters, dark deeds, famous visitors, smuggling, violent vicars, wildlife, past industries and many more tales from Burgh Island and the villages along the Bigbury Bay shoreline are included for your pleasure. You'll be surprised just how much this little book contains!

TEN FAMILY WALKS ON DARTMOOR
Sally and Chips Barber

Ten Family Walks on Dartmoor is designed for the visitor to Dartmoor who wants to get away from it all for just a few hours – a series of sensible strolls that are interesting, include clear but simple maps, and reveal the most beautiful parts of Dartmoor. The walks range from just a few miles up to about 6 or 7 miles in length and are presented in a light and easy-to-read style.

For further details of these or any of our Devon titles, please contact Obelisk Publications, 2 Church Hill, Pinhoe, Exeter EX4 9ER, tel: Exeter 468556.